DNA IS HERE TO STAY

Written by
Dr. Fran Balkwill
Illustrated by
Mic Rolph

HarperCollins*Publishers*

First published in 1992
© text Fran Balkwill 1992
© illustrations Mic Rolph 1992
A CIP catalogue record of this book is available from the British Library
ISBN 0 00 196457 7
ISBN 0 00 196458 5 (PB)

Printed and bound in China
This book is set in Lubalin Graph 13/16

RESOURCE CENTRE
WESTERN ISLES LIBRARIES

Readers are requested to take great care of the books while in their possession, and to point out any defects that they may notice in them to the Librarian.

This book is issued for a period of twenty-one days and should be returned on or before the latest date stamped below, but an extension of the period of loan may be granted when desired.

DATE OF RETURN	DATE OF RETURN	DATE OF RETURN
. . . .	. . . .	. . . .
. . . .	. . . .	. . . .
. . . .	. . . .	. . . .
. . . .	. . . .	. . . .
. . . .	. . . .	. . . .
. . . .	. . . .	. . . .
. . . .	. . . .	. . . .
. . . .	. . . .	. . . .
. . . .	. . . .	. . . .
. . . .	. . . .	. . . .

Once there was a tiny cell, smaller than a grain of sand.
Although that cell was very small it carried an
incredibly complicated and amazingly clever plan....

.....A plan to make a unique living creature....

YOU!

How did that plan fit inside one tiny cell?

ME!

How was it able to put all the parts of you together in the right order? Well, the plan to make you was coiled up in a tangle of very thin threads inside the first cell. To learn about those threads is to learn about the secret of life - the secret of deoxyribonucleic acid (dee-oxy-rye-bow-new-clay-ick-acid). Deoxy..........what? It is such a long word that everyone calls it **DNA**.

5

Through a powerful electron microscope the first cell that was you would look something like this. Where is the DNA?
The DNA is coiled up in the centre of the cell in 46 very long and very thin threads called chromosomes (krome-o-soames).
The threads are so thin that you can't even see them through an electron microscope.

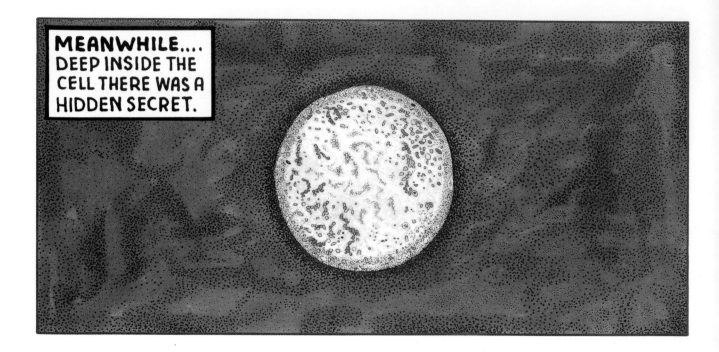

MEANWHILE....
DEEP INSIDE THE
CELL THERE WAS A
HIDDEN SECRET.

But if you unravelled all the DNA from this single cell it would stretch for one and a half metres! And just as difficult to imagine is the width of the DNA threads. You could fit about five million strands through the eye of a needle!

Look closely at the cell now. It is about to divide into two cells.
Can you see dark shapes appearing in the centre of the cell?
These are the chromosome threads. They are full of DNA.

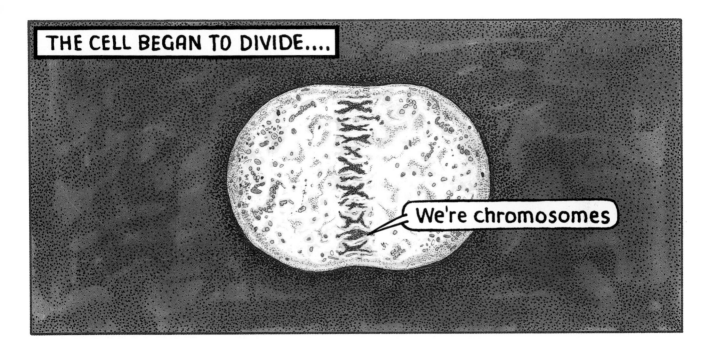

DNA coils up tightly when a cell is about to divide. That is why
you can see the chromosomes. They are shaped a bit like Xs.
All the information needed to make a unique human being is
contained within these chromosomes.

What exactly does DNA look like? We'll unravel the DNA thread from one of the chromosomes. Pretend you've put on some magic glasses that can magnify everything fifty million times. (That would make a grain of sand as big as a mountain!). Now you can easily see one thread of DNA and discover its most important secret.

What a very strange shape

YEAH!

I'M CALLED A DOUBLE HELIX

Not one, but two, strands
make up the DNA thread.
They wind around each other
so that the DNA looks like a
twisting, twirling ladder.
This shape is called
a double helix.

9

Cells are the building blocks of your body. When you were made, a sperm cell with 23 chromosomes fused with an egg cell containing 23 chromosomes and became the first cell that was you.

That first cell then copied its DNA and became two cells with identical plans.

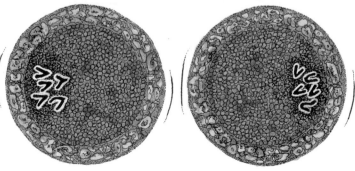

Then two cells became four cells, four cells became eight cells and so on until you were made of millions of cells. And the amazing thing is that each time a cell divided, its DNA plan was copied.

So each of your cells has the same DNA plan
and each of your cells has 46 chromosomes.

How exactly does DNA copy itself?

We'll unravel this DNA strand and find out.

The double helix unzips
so that there are two single strands of DNA.
Then each single strand becomes a pattern for
another strand.
The chemicals that make DNA are floating around
nearby in the cell and join up in a precise order.

The four chemicals are called
Adenine (ad-en-een), **T**hymine
(thy-meen), **C**ytosine (cy-toe-seen),
and **G**uanine (gwa-neen).
We've made each of them a
different colour in the drawing.
They are known by their initials.

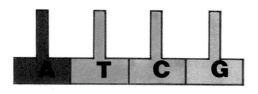

Can you see the order in which the chemicals are joined up?

Look very carefully at the DNA that is being copied in this picture.

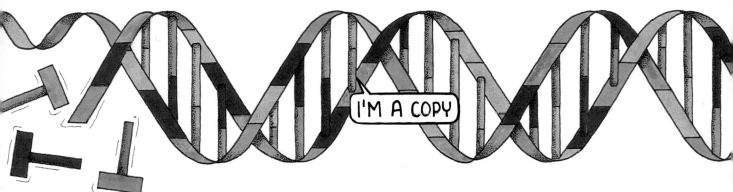

Chemical **A** always joins up with chemical **T**.
Chemical **T** always joins up with chemical **A**.
Chemical **C** always joins up with chemical **G**.
Chemical **G** always joins up with chemical **C**.

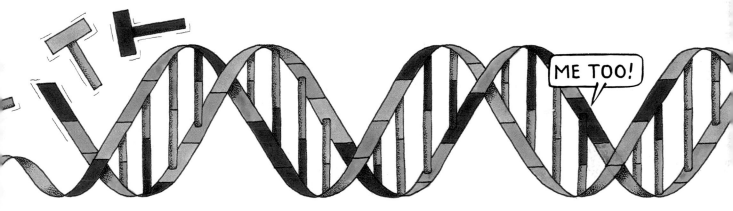

When the copying is finished there are two identical DNA threads in each of the 46 chromosomes – one thread for each of the new cells.

Your DNA plan is like a secret code - a code so complicated that scientists only began to understand as recently as the1940s.
But how does this mysterious, twisting thread actually make you?
Well, it works like this.
Your body is made of cells.
Your cells are made of water, proteins, DNA, sugars, and fats.
DNA is a code for making proteins.

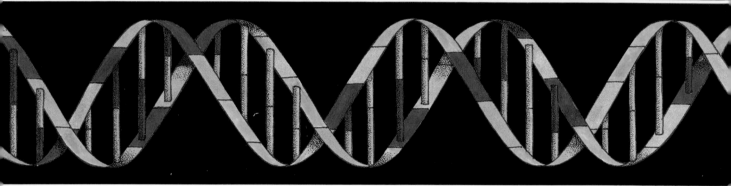

Proteins are important because they help a cell make other chemicals that it needs to do its job. Proteins make cells the shape they are and the colour they are.
Your DNA plan contains recipes for making about fifty thousand different types of proteins.   The recipe for each protein is laid out in order along the DNA threads using the chemicals **A T C G**. Each recipe for a protein is called a gene (jean).

14

So all you have to remember is that
**DNA makes proteins, proteins make cells,
cells make YOU!**

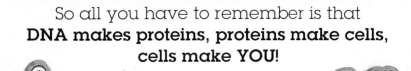

Turn the page to learn about some of your proteins…

Inside your blood cells there is a protein called haemoglobin (heem-o-glow-bin) that carries oxygen around your body.

Cells in your skin make a protein called melanin that gives your skin its particular colour and protects it from ultraviolet rays in sunshine.

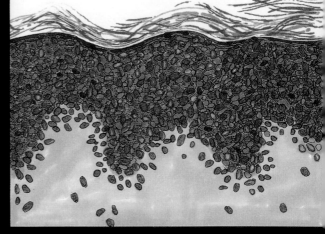

Cells inside your nose make a gloopy protein called mucus that traps germs.

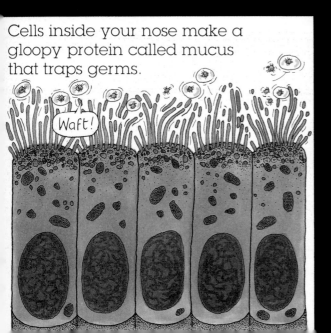

Defender cells make proteins called antibodies that zap invader germs like viruses and bacteria.

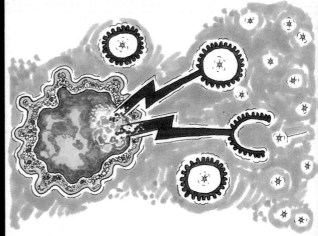

Stomach cells make proteins called enzymes that digest the food you eat into substances that give you energy.

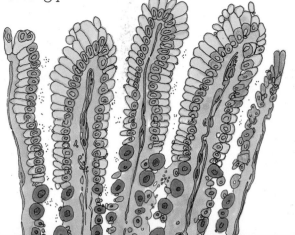

Cells on your head and body make hair. Hair is a protein called keratin.

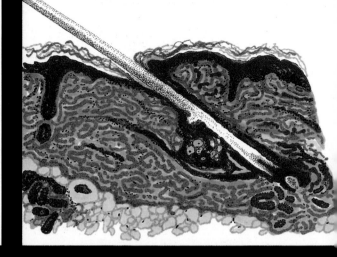

The enamel on the outside of your teeth is a mixture of a protein called collagen and hard crystals of calcium.

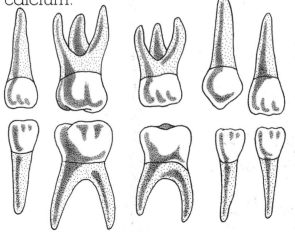

Actin and myosin are slidy proteins that help your muscle cells expand and contract.

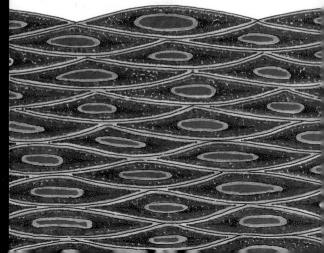

How does DNA act as a code for making these proteins?

To make it easier for you to see, we've straightened out a bit of the double helix. It is a bit complicated, so take a deep breath, concentrate, and remember this strand is magnified about fifty million times! First a small part of the DNA unzips (we'll show you exactly how this happens on page 20.) Now the recipe for a particular protein must be copied from one strand onto another strand.

Deep breath

This is the copy strand

I'm **U**!!

I've Unzipped!

The copy strand looks like a small bit of DNA - with one important difference. One chemical is different.

The copy strand does not use any thymine (**T**), instead it uses a chemical called uracil (your-a-sill) (**U**).

18

As usual, if the DNA strand has a **T**, it copies **A**,
if the DNA strand has a **C** it copies **G**,
if the DNA strand has a **G**, it copies **C**,
but if the DNA strand has an A it copies U.
Nobody knows exactly why this happens.

We'll use a tiny piece of one strand of the DNA
code for the protein haemoglobin to show you
exactly what happens -

The cell makes a copy strand like this.

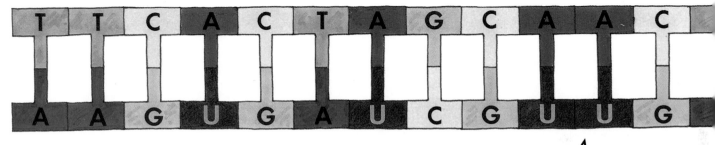

Now here is another bit of the DNA code for
haemoglobin.

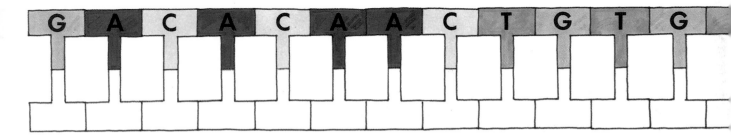

Can you work out what the copy strand will be?

Let's see in more detail how a cell makes the protein haemoglobin.

The gene (recipe) for haemoglobin makes up one tiny part of one of your 46 chromosomes.

That gene becomes unravelled from the rest of the DNA thread and the DNA unzips.

It takes a cell about a minute to make a complete copy of the 1350 **ATC** and **G**s in the gene for haemoglobin.

If we were to write down the complete DNA recipe for haemoglobin at the size it is drawn here, we would need another 36 pages, or 61 metres of paper.

Wow!

Snore!

When the copy
strand is ready it
travels to another area of
the cell to find a ribosome
(rye-bo-soame). The ribosome
is like a microscopic workbench
that holds the copy strand fast.

All proteins are made from
chemicals called amino acids.
The thousands of different proteins
in your body are made from twenty
amino acids joined up together in every
possible combination. The copy strand
has instructions for the particular
combination of amino acids that make
haemoglobin.

The ribosome reads the instructions
on the copy strand. As it moves
along the copy strand it joins
amino acids together like
beads of a necklace.

22

The copy strand is now complete and leaves the chromosome.

The copy strand finds a ribosome (which isn't difficult because there are thousands in each cell).

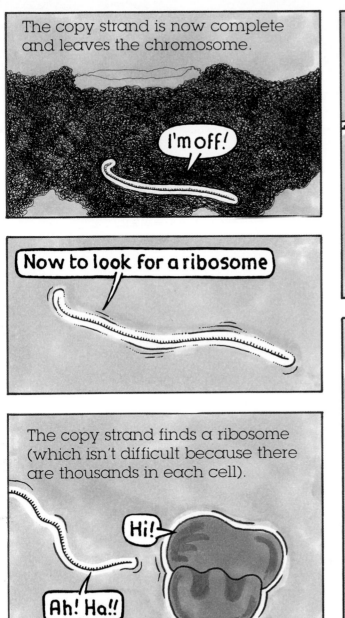

The copy strand sticks to the ribosome which reads the **ACGU**s. Now the ribosome knows the order the amino acids must be joined up in.

And all this happens millions of times a minute, every day, inside the cells of your body.

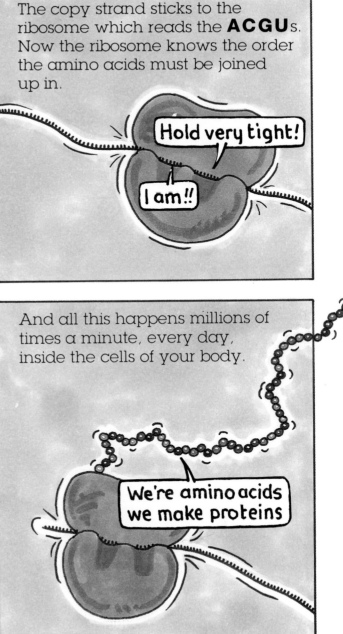

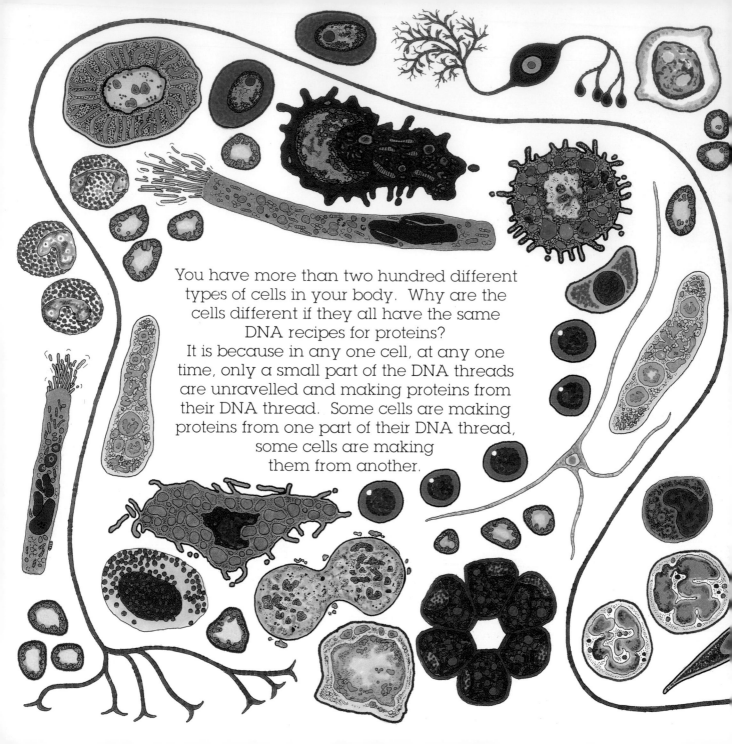

You have more than two hundred different types of cells in your body. Why are the cells different if they all have the same DNA recipes for proteins?
It is because in any one cell, at any one time, only a small part of the DNA threads are unravelled and making proteins from their DNA thread. Some cells are making proteins from one part of their DNA thread, some cells are making them from another.

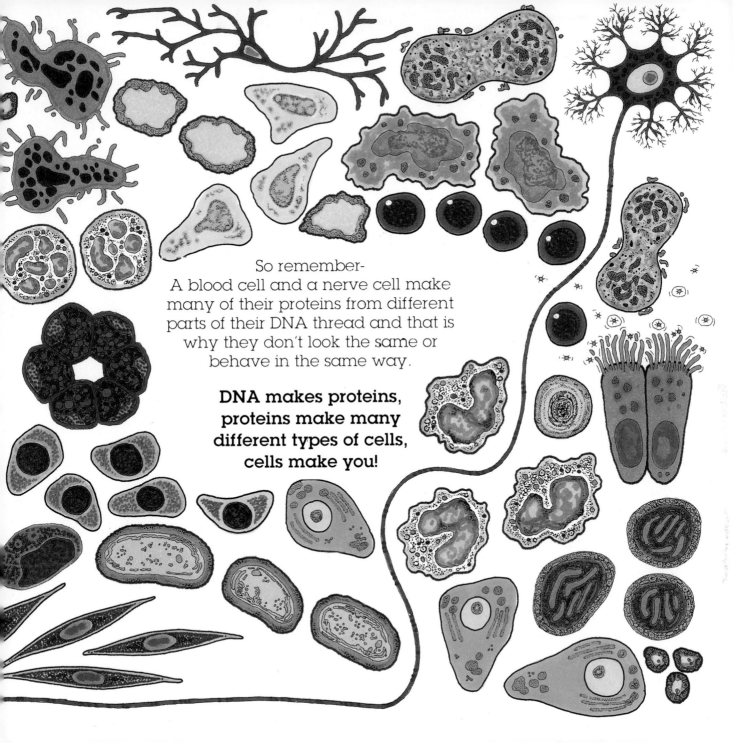

So remember-
A blood cell and a nerve cell make
many of their proteins from different
parts of their DNA thread and that is
why they don't look the same or
behave in the same way.

**DNA makes proteins,
proteins make many
different types of cells,
cells make you!**

Human beings come in all shapes, sizes, and colours, although they are pretty much the same inside. Why do we look different from one another? It is because our DNA plans are all slightly different.

Human DNA is divided into genes which are the recipes for proteins. Many genes make the same proteins in all human beings. In fact, about 99.5% of your DNA is in the same order as everybody else in the world.

But some parts of our DNA plans vary. Your hair colour genes may have recipes for blonde, brown, black or red hair. Genes for eye colour may make them blue, brown, hazel, or green. Genes for skin colour may make you different shades of pink, yellow or brown. We are all slightly different from one another because of the proteins our cells make. And long before you were born, just one tiny part of your DNA, maybe only one gene, first determined whether you were going to be a boy or a girl.

Some illnesses are caused by
mistakes in the DNA plan. These
mistakes mean that a protein is
not made correctly, or is not made
at all. This means that some cells
don't do their jobs properly.
Diseases like cancer, muscular
dystrophy, and cystic fibrosis are
caused by mistakes in DNA.
Scientists all over the world are
trying to unlock the secrets of our
DNA plans in the biggest biology
experiment ever. Computers are
storing a data bank of the
enormous amount of information
in human DNA. Imagine this task
-your DNA threads contain six
thousand million **A T C** and **G**s!
Three thousand million on each
side of the double helix.
Imagine that each one of your 46
chromosomes is a large volume of
an encyclopaedia. On every
page of each volume of this
encyclopaedia would be the
recipes for making all the different
proteins in your body, written
down in millions of **A T C** and **G**'s.

Making a data bank of human DNA will help us to understand the differences between human beings. It will also help us fight disease. If we know where the mistakes are, we might be able to prevent or cure many diseases in the future.

We've told you the story of
human DNA, but there are
millions of other forms of life on this planet,
and millions now extinct. Your body is very different
from a caterpillar or a crab, a killer whale, or a bat.
And (hopefully) you don't look a bit like a spider or a giant tree !
Surely all these living things must have different chemical
plans inside them? But no - the staggering fact is that everything
that lives on the earth has DNA plans that are made of the
same basic chemicals as yours. Their DNA is a double helix
and is made of **A**denine, **T**hymine, **C**ytosine and **G**uanine.
So why doesn't every living thing look and behave the same way?
It is because each species of plant or animal has **A T C G** in a
different order along its DNA. Therefore it makes different proteins,
those proteins make different cells, those cells make different
life forms. And these have all evolved from the first single
cell creatures found three thousand million years ago.
Over millions of years slight mistakes have been made in
copying DNA, and so different species have slowly emerged,
each perfectly adapted to its surroundings.

I suppose you realise
if my DNA had been
in a different order,
I could've been a
brain surgeon!!